Happy

SO-BRP-705

March 97

Teddy Bears

Facts, Trivia & Interesting Stories

From Jack & Sharon

by BETTY O. BENNETT LONG
Revised Edition

Sweet Memories Publishing Company • Smyrna, TN 37167 • 1-615-459-4012

Art Direction & Typography by McClearen Design Studios
3901 Brush Hill Road, Nashville, TN 37216

Edited by Thomas L. Long

ISBN 0-9645218-4-9

PRINTED IN THE UNITED STATES OF AMERICA

PERSONAL DEDICATION

This book is dedicated to my family, friends, fellow bear collectors, beary special bear artists and *Good Bears of the World*.

ACKNOWLEDGMENTS

Special thanks to my husband, for his loving support; to my mother, who keeps the home lights burning while we're away; to our children, who somewhat tolerate our absence, and to all of the bear artists who graciously shared their lives with us.

A special thank you to Betty Frost for her proofreading skills, and to Dan for his ongoing support.

Thanks also to Pioneer Printing of Springfield, Tennessee and McClearen Design for their patience and expertise!

INTRODUCTION

I LOVE TEDDY BEARS! Even though my background mainly consisted of dolls, there has always been a special place in my heart for teddy bears.

Affection for teddy bears is now more than love alone. Many early teddy bears constructed during the Michtom and Steiff period are absolute treasures! Imagine that a teddy bear, made by the Steiff family in 1904, would generate a $171,000 winning bid at a Christies Auction in London. Times change! When I read that story, I thought of all of the teddy bears that are packed away in family attics and trunks.

Realizing that teddy bears are increasing in value, I decided to begin the research for this book to document the facts, trivia and interesting stories associated with teddy bears.

What I have learned is amazing. I have come to understand that teddy bears are very difficult to identify as to manufacturer, year and country of origin. Many early companies simply did not permanently mark each bear. In the United States only two companies ever marked their bears.

The message about teddy bear collecting is simple. Almost every bear is valuable if it has some age and is in very good condition with documented history. Always consult with a local authority or search out the identity of your bear in libraries or within various organizations and museums identified in this book and others.

Now, sit back, relax and enjoy the many intriguing stores that have come to form the basis of this very exciting and valuable hobby.

If you have an interesting fact or anecdote about teddy bears, please send it to me at:

> P.O. Box 414
> Smyrna, TN 37167

> Bear Hugs!

> Betty O. Bennett Long

Q. For what president is the American teddy bear named?
A. Theodore Roosevelt, the 26th President of the United States.

During the fall of 1902, Theodore Roosevelt had scheduled a five-day bear hunt to take place between the borders of Mississippi and Louisiana. Roosevelt had also pledged to resolve an existing border dispute between these two great states between his scheduled hunting excursions.

TR was a great game hunter and had built a reputation regarding his hunting prowess.

During the five-day hunt no one in the presidential party saw any bears until late in the fifth day. The hunting party finally chanced upon a bear and the President raised his trusted rifle to fire. But he could not shoot!

Others in Roosevelt's party raised their guns too. Suddenly the President lowered his gun admonishing the others not to shoot. Did Roosevelt want this prized bear for his own growing trophy wall? Hardly.

Directly in the line of fire was a baby bear, amicably eating the honey that drenched his paws. The golden, caramel colored bear cub continued to enjoy his delectable treat oblivious to the fate that was about to end his life.

Roosevelt held his hand up in a broad, halt fashion and was said to exclaim, "I don't shoot baby bears," and he rode off, ending the bear hunt.

TR's decision not to shoot caught everyone by surprise as he was well known as a fierce and successful game hunter.

Q. In what newspaper did this bear story first appear?
A. *The Washington Post* with a cartoon by staff cartoonist Clifford K. Berryman.

The headline accompanying this story proclaimed, "President Ends Bear Hunt Without A Shot!"

This elicited laughter and grins all over the country.
Soon other newspapers began carrying the cartoon.

Q. What was the cartoon depicting Roosevelt's
   confrontation with a bear called?
A. "Drawing the line in Mississippi."

Also visible in the cartoon were other bears laughing at the
President of the United States. Laughing at the President?

Unmistakably this event caused the development of a new product concept that would warm the hearts of almost every person who gained a friendship with their own "baby bear."

The President's hunting trip proved to be a momentous occasion.

Q. Did Berryman use a bear symbol again originating from this incident?

A. Yes. Clifford drew at least one other version of the original and utilized a bear motif in a number of political cartoons in which he followed the remainder of Roosevelt's presidency.

Along with everyone else in America, a young married Russian immigrant couple living in Brooklyn, New York, saw the headlines and read the stories about the President's hunting trip and the light-hearted commotion it was causing.

The couple was already well-known for their neighbor-hood shop that sold candy, rag dolls, toy ponies, stationery and novelties.

Q. Which married couple is responsible for designing, sewing and displaying the first American teddy bear?

A. Morris Michtom and his wife Rose. They sought to benefit from the new awareness for "baby bears."

Q. Which particular headline gave them the idea to construct a bear similar to that pictured in the news paper cartoon?

A. "The Big Bear Hunt!"

The Michtoms worked on the bear all day. That night the finished bear was placed in the display window of the candy shop.

A mound of chocolate kisses were used to decorate the window along with the bear.

By morning crowds of people stopped to enjoy the new spectacle.

Q. What did the Michtoms name their new friend?
A. "TEDDY" Bear after their affection for the bear shown in the cartoon with the President.

Morris was worried that the President would be insulted to have his name associated with a toy bear and that the President would ask that his name not be used.

He decided to remove the teddy bear from the window and packed it in an old box from his shop.

The next day he mailed the box containing the bear to the White House in Washington, D.C.

Q. What did Morris ask of the President in the note sent with his teddy bear?

A. He asked the President if he could use his name for the new toy idea.

It is said that the President immediately sent the following reply: "The teddy bear now has a name."

Although he could not imagine what good his name would do, he gave the Michtoms permission to use it.

On the day that Morris and Rose received the President's note, they began to make the second bear.

A massive new industry was born. Soon children everywhere began cuddling and sleeping with teddy bears.

Q. Which toy wholesaler quickly approached the Michtoms about distributing and selling their popular new product known as "Teddy's bear"?

A. Butler Brothers, then one of the largest toy wholesalers in the United States.

The Butler Brothers also underwrote the credit needs of the Michtoms with their raw material suppliers so that Morris and Rose could meet the escalating demand for the bears.

Q. In what year, and what election for president was a teddy bear used on every campaign button?

A. In 1904 during Theodore Roosevelt's reelection campaign.

Any one of the campaign buttons from that campaign is a treasured collectible. It is a small campaign button with TR, his running mate Fairbanks, and the now famous Berryman cartoon bear. The bear is shown holding a flag that says "Four More Years of Theodore."

Q. What year did TR pass out teddy bears on the back of his train?

A. In 1904. History states that these bears were made by the Ideal Toy Company.

Q. Where is Morris and Rose Michtom's first teddy bear located today?

A. The first teddy bear is on display in the Smithsonian Institution in Washington, D.C.

Prompted by a letter to the Michtoms from Roosevelt's daughter, Kermit, the first "teddy" was given a place of honor in a glass case at The National Archive.

Q. What happened to Morris and Rose Michtom's company after the success with the first teddy bear?

A. Formed in 1903 as Ideal Novelty and Toy Company, it produced all of the Morris Michtom bears in conjunction with the financing provided the company by the Butler Brothers. Years later the company came to be known as The Ideal Toy Company.

Shoppers in 1923 probably recognized the Ideal company by its slogan: "When we do it, we do it right," later to become "Excellence in toy making since the teddy bear."

Q. Who really coined the term "teddy bear"?
A. Although Michtom claims to have written Roosevelt requesting to use his first name as a variation on the bear as "Teddy," no record has ever been produced that shows Michtom's letter nor Roosevelt's famed hand-written reply.

As an interesting aside, Teddy Roosevelt admitted to the value of the bear surviving in its natural environment but is never known to have uttered or written the words "teddy bear."

Q. Did Roosevelt continue to align himself with the bear image?
A. Yes. For the rest of his career, Roosevelt capitalized on the event and used the bear as his motif and mascot.

In the 1912 presidential campaign, the incumbent William Howard Taft ran as a Republican. Theodore Roosevelt, directly responsible for the rousing development of the teddy bear concept, had bolted the republican party in that same year. He then started the Progressive Party. Wilson won, but the continuing direct link between Roosevelt and the teddy bear were affirmed.

Due to the link between Teddy Roosevelt and the "Teddy" bear, the Michtoms were credited with making the first teddy bear in America.

Q. Who was the famous German maker of teddy bears?
A. Margarete Steiff.

Q. When was she born?
A. 1847.

Until the creation of the family teddy bear, the Steiffs' most popular product had been a stuffed-elephant pin cushion.

Margarete suffered from childhood polio which left her legs permanently paralyzed and dramatically weakened her left arm.

Eager to be independent and wanting to earn her own living she learned to sew.

She later became a well-known seamstress in the town of Giëngen-am-Brenz in the area of Wurtemburg where she resided.

She made a living selling clothes that she made from felt materials that she got from her uncle's felt factory. Later, in her teen years, she opened a dress shop.

From that dress shop, Margarete developed the pin cushions. Soon she was designing, selling and displaying other stuffed animals. These included horses, pigs, monkeys, donkeys and camels.

By 1893 she exhibited her product line at the prestigious Leipzig Toy Fair.

Q. Who caused Margarete Steiff to develop her first teddy bear?

A. Her nephew Richard, based on his studying of bear sculptures in Stuttgart.

Richard also had a fanciful eye for the antics of bear cubs at the zoo and in the Hagenbech Circus.

Q. What year did Richard join the Steiff company?

A. 1879.

Many years later Richard designed bears that incorporated movable heads and limbs. He also dressed his bears. Margarete was not impressed as she had made her bears stand on all fours or pose as upright dancing bears.

Margarete's bears were not very successful until Richard's ideas were presented and accepted by her.

Q. In what year was the new Steiff styled bear shown to the public?
A. In 1903 at the Leipzig Toy Fair.

Before that eventful day, another of Steiff's nephews, Paul Steiff, left for America to create interest in the product. He failed.

Most Americans thought the prototype too thick, fat and clumsy, calling it a "stuffed misfit."

Q. Which New York toy importer bought the Steiff bear for import into the United States?

A. George Borgfeldt and Company.

A buyer from Borgfeldt commented to the Steiffs how "empty the fair was for something new, something soft and something cuddly."

Richard Steiff produced a new-styled bear incorporating the suggestions he heard in America.

The response? An immediate order for 3000 bears.

American response was so favorable that the order was doubled and by the end of 1903 Steiff had sold over 12,000 bears in America.

Q. How many bears were the Steiffs producing by 1907?
A. 974,000 bears.

The Steiffs proclaimed that year as "Bärenjahre," or Year of the Bear!

Q. Who then is thought to be the first inventor of the modern-day teddy bear?
A. That honor is shared among historians of teddy bear facts and trivia as a tossup between the Michtoms of America and the Steiffs of Germany.

Q. What was the original Steiff bear known as, if not teddy?

A. As a German bear it had a German name, "Petz."

Q. What are the distinguishing characteristics of a true Steiff bear?

A. Featuring the recognizable humped back and elongated nose, the Steiff bear is readily identifiable.

Finding a small metal button bearing the Steiff name fixed to the left ear will support your find as a Steiff.

In 1904, Margarete Steiff pledged to her customers that every bear she made would be identified by a small nickel button fixed to the left ear.

Steiff applied for its registration mark on December 20, 1904 with the registration officially taking effect on May 13, 1905.

Q. What are some other tell-tale marks that distinguish a Steiff?

A. Older Steiffs have a smaller button with Roman letters spelling S-T-E-I-F-F. This signifies an older bear if compared to one whose button prints Steiff in basic script.

Sometimes the recognizable Steiff tag also dates the manufacture period. Look for buttons made of pewter or pewter mixes to date the bear.

Also, chrome or high-polished metal predate the later bears.

Q. How can you distinguish the colored tag sometimes found on a Steiff?
A. Before 1926 look for white labels. Red labels were used from 1926 to 1934.

Yellow followed from 1934 on. White and yellow, and black and white tags were used starting with 1980 and continue today.

Less information on the tag usually indicates an older Steiff.

Steiff maintains four factories today: two in West Germany, one in Austria and one in Tunisia.

Steiff also maintains a museum at Giëngen-am-Brenz in West Germany. A pure delight awaits the true teddy bear collector as hundreds of original bears, dolls and animals are displayed in mint condition.

Margarete Steiff died in Grengon, Germany in 1909.

Q. Why do we continually cherish teddy bears?
A. To show affection and the spirit of love to a cute, cuddly, innocent and lovable baby bear.

Q. What manufacturer made the first electric, bright-eyed teddy bear and when?
A. Bruin Manufacturing Company, in 1907.

During that year, to the surprise of many, the Bruin Company developed and produced the "Electric Bright-Eyed Teddy Bears."   When the right paw was moved up and down, the bear's eyes would light up in either white or red.

These bears are identified by a woven label printed with B.M.C. stitched across the bottom of the right foot.

Q. What company was the first to offer products bearing the image of the newly popular teddy bears?

A. The Lloyd Manufacturing Company produced and sold teddy bear carts and cages.

The Lloyd Manufacturing Company, located in Menominee, Michigan, announced "the best selling novelty of the year." This turned out to be the carts and cages.

Leo Shlesinger began offering teddy bear pails and tea sets constructed of light metals painted in very bright colors.

Pedal cars were soon advertised with plush teddy bears behind the wheel.

Next came a popular teddy bear hammock made of canvas followed by the teddy bear squeeze ball. Soon many products emerged to include: Teddy bear targets, paper dolls, party games, penny banks, blocks, wagons, scarf pins, rubber stamps, water pistols and more. Scores of post cards soon began to make a debut.

Q. During 1906, how many goats were sheared per week to generate wool for use in making teddy bears by the Tinque Manufacturing Company?

A. Four thousand goats.

Q. What type of plush was used to make teddy bears before World War I?

A. Mohair plush.

Before World War I teddy bears were designed to be very bear-like, that is, they had true-to-life humped backs, pointed muzzles and long limbs. Many had felt pads on the paws and feet. Shoe buttons were used as eyes.

American teddy bears evolved differently from their cousins manufactured in Great Britain or Germany, the two other manufacturing centers.

Q. What was the visual difference between European and American teddy bears?
A. The British versions had flatter faces, shorter, straighter limbs and eventually no humped back.

Also during this period the shape of the teddy bear was changing dramatically.

Q. By 1911 how were the paws and feet stitched?
A. The paws and feet were stitched vertically with four stitches on each paw and each foot.

Q. By 1913 what were the eyes usually made of?
A. Wood, felt, metal shoe buttons, leather and clear glass
   eyes painted black.

Q. In which year did we first see manufacturers using
   rolling glass eyes set in sockets?
A. 1922.

Q. By 1934 what were manufacturers using to make eyes for teddys?

A. Many used bulbous opaque glass, enameled metal buttons, amber, black glass and blue glass.

Q. Before 1940 what was the traditional fiber being used to stuff teddy bears?

A. Excelsior.

Q. By 1940 what type of fibers were used to stuff teddy bears?

A. Usually kapok.

By 1940, the outer fabric of many teddy bears was made of new synthetic fibers resulting in less realistic coloring of the fur.

Q. What is the best indicator as the approximate age of a teddy bear?

A. The eyes.

It is difficult to distinguish glass eyes from plastic.
However, placing your lips directly on the eye will give you
a hint as to the material. Glass will feel colder and harder
than other materials. Glass eyes indicate an older bear.

Teddy bear noses were often stitched with thread. The
more unusual were made of celluloid, tin and leather, and
often date before World War I.

Q. In what year did manufacturers begin using a rectangular stitching for the nose?
A. 1945.

The first unjointed teddy bear appeared in 1947.

Q. In which year did United States manufacturers begin using plastic and rubber for the noses?
A. About 1953.

The majority of the mouths were stitched with black or brown threads forming what has come to be known as the traditional "V" shape. The Michtoms started this.

Variations of this approach enabled other teddy bears to gain different expressions.

Teddy bear claws were often styled in various materials. Some of the more unusual teddys have the claws carved in wood or molded in hard rubber. Over the years these parts have deteriorated and the concept has been lost.

Q. Who was the first manufacturer to make a teddy bear with a hinged jaw?

A. Knickerbocker Toy Company.

Q. Who made the "Buddy Teddy Bear" in 1932?

A. The Ideal Toy Company.

Q. The "Teddy-Boy" and "Teddy-Girl" teddy bears are a sequel to what?

A. The Travels and Adventures of the Roosevelt Bears.

Q. Who is often identified as the first collector of teddy bears?

A. Mary Hillier began collecting teddy bears in Britain during the 1920's.

Q. How many bears were thought to be in existence in the U.S. by 1964?

A. 140 million

In Great Britain it is estimated that over 60 percent of all households are occupied by a teddy bear.

Q. What accounts for the staying power of teddy bears as safe, cuddly toys?

A. Theories abound, but one of the most heralded originates as to timing. Teddy Bears came to market when there was a definable need for toys to be clung to by boys. Dolls were considered unsuitable and unmanly. Facts point to teddy bears being acceptable to boys as well as to girls. One reason for the continuing bear-boy relationship may be that the teddy bear is gender neutral. It seems to be neither male or female unless dressed in a particular fashion.

A teddy bear is deemed "tougher" than a doll. A teddy bear can be treated with affectionate toughness--like a friend.

A teddy bear is also a comforter--an extension of the security blanket. Psychologists have recognized it as a father figure appealing to childhood goodness, benevolence and kindness.

The famed British teddy bear collector and authority, Colonel Robert Henderson, described the power of teddy bears in a 1977 article in *Bear Track* magazine:

".....from early times the bear has commanded a special place in folklore, myth, fairy-tale and legend. It has been regarded as a representative of both divine and natural forces; and today, in the form of the teddy bear, it is grasped in psychic compensation and clung to for security. The reason for this is that the bear functions as a powerful symbol that provides satisfaction for a widespread psychological need. Consequently, history, religion, philosophy and psychology are all involved in any proper explanation of the teddy bear."

In summation, Colonel Henderson says that the teddy bear "plays a great part in the psychological development of many people of all ages all over the world. This is because he is a truly international figure that is non-religious and yet is universally recognized as a symbol of love and affection. He represents friendship."

Q. Does Great Britain have a famous teddy bear story too?
A. Yes.

It seems King Edward VII took a liking to an Australian koala bear kept at the London Zoo. It became known as "Teddy's Bear" in his honor. It was then easy for the Brits to claim the same name for the stuffed teddy bears that were beginning to show up in stores and with young children.

It is also thought to be named as "a put-off about King Edward's mistress, Lillie Langtry, who pampered her 'teddy bear,' which in this case was the king."

Later Britain adopted the term teddy bear.

Q. What year did the first ad for teddy bears appear in
the US toy magazine *Playthings*?

A. May 1906.

The ad described a range of "jointed plush bears" but did
not use the full term--teddy bears.

In November of that year, E.I. Horseman ran an ad in
Playthings describing the product as "Teddy Bears."

Q. Did the Horseman ad refer to teddy bears as plush, cuddly teddy bears?

A. No, only to the bear-shaped automobile accessories used as toys.

It was not until December 1906 that the actual term "teddy bear" was applied to the plush characters still referred to only as "Teddy's" bears.

Q. What did these teddy bears wholesale at?
A. "Imported teddy bears--best quality with voice--
$4.50 to $72 per dozen."

In 1907, a New York importer L. H. Mace and Company
offered a wholesale catalog depicting "plush" teddy bears.
This was the first known use of the term "plush" to
describe the teddy bear product.

Webster and Oxford dictionaries identified the term
"teddy bear" in 1907.

Q. Which years have been identified as the period when teddy bears as we know them today came into existence?

A. 1906 and 1907, in America and Germany.

Q. When did manufacturers begin putting clothes on teddy bears?

A. By 1906, two American companies, Kahn & Mossbacher and W. Shoyer & Company were in competition with a full range of clothes for the "well-dressed" teddy bear.

Q. What was the earliest known advertisement for teddy bears in Great Britain?

A. In 1909, a Christmas advertisement for Morsells of Oxford Street.

This ad featured the "Old Mistress" teddy bear that "lived in a shoe."

Many of the early British bears were actually made by Steiff and imported from Germany.

Q. Who was the first known manufacturer of plush
   teddy bears in Great Britain?
A. J.K. Fornell and Company.

This company had been known for making stuffed
animals from natural skins, however, they made their
teddys from plush manufactured in Yorkshire.

The Fornell factory was destroyed by fire in 1934.

Q. After Fornell burned did it rebuild?
A. Yes. Then one of the directors left and started a competing company called "Merrythought."

Many thought the Fornell bear was built on a Steiff model. Some believe that a passive licensing agreement may have been signed between the two companies.

Teddy bears were now a growing item on both sides of the Atlantic with the United States, Germany and Great Britain feeding the demand.

Teddy bears were now fully accepted by the people of all countries, and toy products, gift products and wheel products began using bears to create interest for the products bearing the likeness.

Q. Who owns the largest known collection of teddy bears in the U.S.?
A. Matt Murphy of Texas who is a banker.

Q. How many bears in his collection?
A. 1,317, collected from 135 different manufacturers.

Q. What term is used to define a collection of teddy
bears?
A. "HUG."

Victor Davis of San Francisco has a hug of over 800 bears.

Virginia Walker of Florida enjoys over 600 bears in her
hug.

Robin Castro of Nashville, Tennessee, has a hug of over 350 bears including over 100 Panda Bears, starting with the first bear given her as a baby by her grandparents.

Q. Who had the largest collection of teddy bears in Great Britain?
A. Colonel Robert Henderson of Edinburgh.

Q. Who is identified with owning the smallest collectible teddy bear in the world?
A. Colonel Henderson.

His collection contains a bear 1/3 inch (8.5 mm) high that may be the smallest documented collector bear.

Q. In 1926, who owned the J.K. Fornell bear, now owned by a New York Library?

A. A. A. Milne, author of the Winnie the Pooh series.

Q. In what year was the Chad Valley Bear introduced?

A. In 1924 in Britain. The Chad Valley Bear is known for its very rare "wine" colors.

It utilized a button in the ear similar to the method employed by the Steiffs.

Chad Valley started making soft toys and dolls during World War I because German products could not be imported.

They also owned the teddy bear company, ISSA Works.

Chad Valley produced teddy bears in six different qualities and thirteen sizes.

Chad Valley bears "growled" due to being fitted with a patented "Chad Valley Growler."

If you think you have a Chad Bear look for the ear tag button similar to a Steiff.

The tag reads: "Chad Valley British Hygienic Toys."

Q. Are there teddy bears available that are classified as antiques?

A. No. Antiques are usually at least 100 years old. The oldest teddy bears available today got their start in the very early 1900's, making the oldest teddy bear about 92 years old. It will be into the next century before a teddy bear can be rightly classified as an antique! Even though this is true, bears over 50 years old are often referred to as antiques.

This factor gives a greater value to existing collections as access to and ownership of classic and valuable teddy bears are readily available to anyone.

Visiting museums would be a great way to get a look at some of these "old" bears.

The Bear Museum of Petersfield has a wonderful collection of old bears including, a large section dedicated to mechanical bears.

It is owned by Judy and John Sparrow, who paid over $6000 for a Steiff bear to become the centerpiece of the museum.

Q. Which price is reported as the most ever paid for a teddy bear?

A. $171,000 for a teddy bear which belonged to the Colonel Henderson collection.

This bear was a Steiff cinnamon plush bear and sold at a Christies Auction on December 5, 1994 in London.

Colonel Henderson was a renowned arctophile. Prior to his death in 1990, he ran the UK branch of the Good Bears of the World. During World War II, Colonel Henderson served as Small Arms Advisor to Field Marshall Montgomery at the time of the D-Day landing at Normandy.

The buyer of the $171,000 teddy bear was identified as Yoshihiro Sekiguchi, a 48-year-old president of the Arrow Toy Company of Japan.

The bear known as "Teddy-Girl" generated Sekiguchi's final bid based upon its provenance (or record as to history) proving its early age.

The bear was actually produced at Steiff in 1904, one year after Steiff produced its first jointed plush bear.

The gender of this bear (Teddy-Girl) changed as a direct result of the birth of the Colonel's daughter in 1942. When Henderson presented his cherished bear to his daughter, he encouraged it to be renamed "Teddy-Girl."

Sekiguchi plans to open a major toy and teddy bear museum in Izu, Japan. "Teddy-Girl," the name given to Colonel Henderson's teddy bear, will be the center of attention at the museum.

Q. What is an "arctophile"?
A. An arctophile is a person who collects teddy bears.

Q. Which other bears brought a high price at the Christies Auction?

A. A Steiff, 1910 circa golden mohair, 19-inch bear brought approximately $3,750.

Another 19-inch bear named "Rupert," also a Steiff, garnered $3,100 at the auction.

A third bear identified as a 13-inch, 1904 Steiff black, plush teddy bear was sold for $34,100.

The entire lot of bears that were sold as part of the Christies Auction brought a total of over $450,000.

Over 500 bears sold at that auction belonged to the collection of Colonel Henderson.

Japanese collectors continue to buy huge selections of older teddy bears for their personal collections.

Have you checked an attic or old family trunk for a teddy bear lately? Because of its relatively recent beginning, the collecting of teddy bears is a valuable and rewarding endeavor that will last well into the future.

Q. How can a novice or experienced collector ensure that a bear is old and worthy of paying a higher price?

A. The bear's fur must be studied first.

The earliest bears were made of mohair. Others used leather, blanket material--usually wool and scrap patches similar to those in an old quilt.

Study the limbs next. Longer arms, often extending midway down the leg, signify an older bear. Watch for curved arms that point the paw up and away from the body.

Early bears are recognized by their extra large feet, often cocked at right angles to the leg. Narrow ankles follow a tapered design.

Also, older bears are known for their very discernible humps. Any signs of the hump as part of the design may point to extra value.

Most pre-1915 teddy bears can be identified by the black button eyes used almost exclusively up to that time.

Original eyes tend to be securely attached to the bear's head and cannot be easily moved with your fingers.

Later thread-connected eyes can be moved in this manner.

Q. What is a "Bing" bear?
A. Bing bears were first identified as being mechanical bears that walk, climb and tumble with clock-like precision. These plush bears were made over a strong metal form and were marketed in the early 1900's.

Bing bears were identified by a metal tag marked G.B.N. until 1919.

If the original tag is still attached, you have a very rare find.

An 8-inch Bing bear survived the sinking of the Titanic.
It was owned by Gaspare Luigi Gatti, an Italian who was
the ship's restaurant manager. The bear had been given to
Gatti by his son just prior to his departure aboard the
Titanic and was returned to the Gatti family along with
other personal items, including a favorite pipe.

The Bing bear owned by Gatti now rests in the Museum
of Childhood in Lancashire, England.

This museum offers its visitors over 250,000 items of
interest, including bears, dolls, doll houses and more.

Q. What are the primary features of a "Hermann" bear?
A. Early examples are rare and include excellent mohair sewn in multiple tones and filled with excelsior.

Hermann used both glass and shoe-button eyes. Many have a strong similarity to Steiff bears, so you should seek a trained expert before you buy!

Q. What is a "Merrythought" bear?
A. Beginning as a manufacturer of mohair products, Merrythought began making soft toy products, including bears, when it lost the business of its largest customer for mohair. These English bears can be identified by tags that are both printed and embroidered.

Merrythought produced 5000 fully jointed mohair replicas of Gatti's bear to commemorate the 80th anniversary of the Titanic's sinking.

Q. Who made the Chiltern bear?
A. H.G. Stone, who got his start at J.K. Fornell, and
   L. Rees founded H.G. Stone Company in 1920.

It is located in Childton Hills of Buckinghamshire where
the Chiltern name was formally registered in 1924.

The early Chiltern bears had cloth feet with stick-on
labels.

Q. What is the Dean's Rag Book Company, Ltd.?
A. As a recognized manufacturer of virtually
   indestructible rag books, Dean produced its first
   teddy bear in 1905. The first bear was actually
   one of the first "kits" offered for teddy bears.

Dean's first plush teddy bear was produced in 1917.

Q. What are "Stearnsy" bears?
A. Started in a hardware store in Stott's City, Missouri, in 1916, Stearnsy bears are often referred to as the most human-like of any teddy bear. They are fully jointed and are modeled after people known by the Stearns.

Sally Stearns started the company after buying three old teddy bears at an antique store, redressing them in old clothes, and giving them names.

The Stearnsy bears range in size from 4 to 22 inches with each bear name-tagged with information about it.

The two most popular, longest lived and lovable bears in literature were inspired by teddy bears bought at "Herrods and Selfridges" in London.

These bears are now known as "Winnie-The-Pooh" and "Paddington Bear."

Pooh's leading illustrator, Ernest Shepard, gained additional information and insight for his illustrations of Winnie-the-Pooh by using a Steiff bear belonging to his son.

The first Winnie-the-Pooh book was published in 1926 and became so popular that it has even been printed in Latin.

It was of course authored by A. A. Milne.

As A. A. Milne's book, *Winnie-The-Pooh* grew in
popularity it came to be recognized by Walt Disney. On
June 16, 1961, Disney decided to add the bear to his
growing list of characters. On that day, and for the next
three years, he committed the talents of a director, six
writers, eleven animators, nine "voices," three background
artists, four layout artists and two composers. Together
they rewrote, redrew and re-storied the Milne book. In
total, over 150 Disney people were involved in producing
a twenty-six minute film called "Winnie-The-Pooh and
the Honey Tree."

Q. Who made the first Paddington Bear?
A. Shirley Clarkson of Gabrielle Designs. She and her husband Eddie showed this bear at the Nuremburg Toy Fair and sales grew dramatically.

Michael Bond created Paddington Bear in 1958. His book earned the "Best Children's Book of 1958" distinction in that year. This was the first book about a teddy bear to do so.

Q. Are any of the early Winnie-The-Pooh bears valuable?
A. Yes. A limited edition of 2,500 Winnie-The-Pooh bears produced in 1986-87 are scarce and desirable. The 18-inch bear features a label in the leg seam and a hang tag. Many place their value at $1200 each.

Q. Besides the Steiffs, what are some other teddy bears identified as valuable?
A. Wilhelm Strunz produced a 15-inch beige mohair teddy bear around 1907 that is very valuable.

It featured shoe-button eyes, black embroidered nose and claws and a red embroidered mouth. The unmarked bear is usually dressed in a policeman's outfit (an English Bobby). It is usually valued in the $2500 range.

A Bing bear, 12 inches high with felt pads, shoe-button eyes and excelsior stuffing, with a right-side key winding, produced in 1908, is valued at $4000.

"Gilbert," a rare Steiff "Bear-Dolly" teddy bear, made in 1912, sold at an earlier Christies Auction for $16,000, showing again the value many are placing on early bears.

This bear is only 12 inches tall. The bear does have a hump, a swivel-head and the tell-tale elongated arms.

"Gilbert" was produced especially for the American presidential elections of 1912 and sold under the name "Dolly-Bear."

Q. How many sizes of this bear were produced?
A. Three sizes: 13, 12 and 10 inch.

Q. What are "Antiseptic" bears?
A. "Antiseptic" bears have common characteristics with features that tend to be exaggerated. These bears have large humps on their backs, long noses, long arms, long thin feet and large set-back ears.

The Miller Antiseptic bear is usually found in beige and in white and was probably made during 1906 to 1907.

Many references to teddy bears are found in the letters and advertisements produced during World War II.

Magazine advertisements produced during this period often used teddy bears to brighten up an otherwise grim subject matter.

The Red Cross and others used the teddy bear in many ads seeking support for the war. Soldiers often mentioned their gratefulness to the U.S.O. and the Red Cross for forwarding these ads to them on the front.

In 1979, *The London Sunday Mirror* held a letter-writing competition to find its readers' best stories about teddy bears in World War II.

One soldier wrote: "Teddys never flinch from danger...in emergencies, when you feel the need for a beloved object and constant moral support, it's nice to know it's on tap...there is a steady quality about a teddy bear..his serene composure can often bring a sense of proportion back and make you realize what the important things in life are and aren't...again there is concrete proof that a state of mind can be inspired by the companionship of a teddy bear!"

It now seems that teddy bears with a unique history, documented as to ownership and manufacturer, rise steadily in value. Many antique dolls do not even come close to the values of these relatively "new" bears.

The development of teddy bears has dramatically increased the interest of collectors about early teddy bears and the people who were responsible for the concept.

From time to time you may need to repair a favorite or valuable teddy bear. You may check with: The Dolls' Hospital, 1787 Lexington Avenue, New York, NY 10021.

The following information identifies the Teddy Bear Artists Association.

The TBAA is a professional association dedicated to the protection, advancement and the professionalization of teddy bear artists through communication and caring. The TBAA was formed in 1991 to provide a consistent center of communication to answer questions, resolve

problems and promote activities within the world of teddy bears.

TBAA members include artists, hobbyists, store owners, promoters, collectors, suppliers and other arctophiles.

You may contact the TBAA by writing:

Teddy Bear Artists Association
P.O. Box 905
Woodland Hills, CA 91365

CONTEMPORARY BEAR
ARTISTS

A special "thank you" goes to Lisa Scroggins and Millie Gage for putting me in touch with these artists.

I can honestly say I have never had the pleasure of getting to know a more caring group of people in my entire life. I enjoyed talking to each and every one of you and I truly admire the wonderful work you do. Thank you for sharing your life and your bear photos with us. I sincerely wish you all the very best!

Due to space limitations, I was unable to list the many awards and accomplishments of these wonderful artists. They are truly amazing!

Betty O. Bennett Long

DONNA BJERKE

About 15 years ago, Donna found herself with two children in school, a husband with a good job, and time on her hands to do anything she wanted. Since her best friend Bonnie was in the same situation, they gathered up all of the projects they had worked on all winter and participated in their first craft show in Jay, Vermont.

In the next few months Donna did a few more shows and observed that the people who were doing well had focused on one particular subject. She went to a local craft store and looked through patterns and found a bear. It was a simple pattern, unjointed but wonderful.

In the years that followed, she worked to perfect her new found love. She made other items, but all were bear related. Teddy evolved in the next few years. She started using better fur and worked on the look in his face and made him fully jointed.

"I consider myself very fortunate because deep in my heart, I know I am doing what the good Lord intended for me to do on on this Earth!"

Bjerke Ltd.
RR1, Box 1117
Charlotte, VT 05445
802-425-2270

RITA CASEY

As a mother of eleven children, grandmother of twenty-three, and great-grandmother of one, Rita has had quite a bit of sewing experience over the years.

She has been making bears, dolls and other animals as a hobby and for gifts for the past forty years. She has been concentrating on teddy bears for the past eight years.

She began with porcelain and sculptured dolls. It was when she really started focusing on bears, that Rita discovered how much she loved making them, talking to people about them, and teaching others how to make quality bears.

In July 1992, Rita and her husband opened a shop in Fairport, New York. Their shop represents bears from over ninety artists as well as a variety of manufactured bears.

Their company motto is: "What is created with love is cherished."

"All of this has given me a tremendous amount of joy and happiness!"

Casey Creations
17 Lodge Pole Road
Pittsford, NY 14534
716-425-3566

HOLLY DYER

Holly started making bears in 1979 as Christmas gifts for her family. Several years later she bought the Biolosky book on bear making and tried it out. Holly and her mother designed a Bee Bear patterned after a sticker sent by a friend. He was made of black velvet, had felt wings, gold velvet stripes and feelers, and was smelling a flower. They liked him so much they made another one in acrylic fur, and the first Watersmith bear was born. He is her logo bear today.

Many more bears came after that; most were traditional in style. One of the most popular now is the "Timothy" family. They range in size from 3 1/2 to 23 1/2 inches.

Holly travels to a wide range of teddy bear shows and conventions. She was the featured guest speaker at the Hug-In in Toronto, Canada. She was also invited to the first Disneyland Teddy Bear Classic in 1992.

"One of the best things about this business is the many friends you can make along the way. I have many close friends I met through bears. I really enjoy this business!"

Hollybearys
203 S. Water St.
P O Box 139
Mt. Blanchard, OH 45867-0139
419-694-5301

REBECCA FIELDS

Rebecca is a relatively new artist, having made her very first bear just two years ago for her nephew. When she looked into the face of her first bear, she was hooked. Although her first attempts were a little mousy, they soon developed into the more respectable bears she had pictured in her mind.

At that time, Rebecca was working in aerospace and knew that, due to downsizing, her job would end the following summer. Suddenly, she was no longer in a quandary over what to do from there.

Rebecca crafts each of her bears individually, with a different characteristic.

Some have eyelids, some have flexlimbs, tongues and claws. Some are stuffed with excelsior, polyfil, beads, or a combination. Even though it is common practice for an artist to develop a trademark, Rebecca would rather not be limited to a certain look.

Rebecca considers herself very lucky to be a part of the bear world. "I have found bear artists to be very friendly and genuine people. I have made friendships at bear shows that will last a lifetime."

Griscom-Townsend Recollections
76 Sparks Avenue
Pennsville, NJ 08070
609-678-5434

KIMBERLY FISCHER

Kimberly began making bears in 1990. Her grandmother had a very serious heart attack that required triple bypass surgery. As part of recovery, heart patients are required to use something soft and weighted for therapy. Kimberly decided to try to make a teddy bear for her from a piece of mohair and a pattern she had bought.

After learning the mechanics of bear making, Kimberly started drawing her own patterns. Through trial and error, she eventually formed a look that distinguished her bears from other artists' bears. She began making her own bears as a way of supplementing her income. She soon learned that it was very difficult to be a "part-time" bear artist and had to make a career choice. This was a difficult decision for her, as she had been training to be a dance teacher since childhood. Eventually, the bears won and a new career adventure was started.

Kimberly designs and makes each of her bears herself. She has never kept any of her own bears. She would rather share her special friends with other family members to comfort them through a rough time.

Kimberly's Bearied Treasure ®
1 Central Ave. & W. Broadway
Haledon, NJ 07508
201-595-1451

ROBIN L. FOLEY

As an illustrator for several Fortune 500 companies and with college training in textiles, creating original sculptured and sewn creatures seemed a logical union for Robin Foley. She made her first bears in 1990 for her baby daughter. Robin focused entirely on bears for the first three years. At times she found she needed more of an artistic challenge. Bunnies were her first attempt to venture beyond bears. This seemed to invite special requests for more challenging animals like koalas, penguins and foxes. This was a perfect opportunity to begin experimenting with fully articulated armatures, and allowed for animals that looked a little more realistic than toy-like.

Currently, she is sculpting fourteen endangered animal species for a gallery show that will debut in July of 1996. A portion of the proceeds will benefit the breeding programs for these animals.

Robin Foley's biggest challenge is to continue to create fresh and exciting pieces while managing the business side of Rag-O-Muffins.

Rag-O-Muffins
2917 SW Fairview Blvd.
Portland, OR 97201
503-222-5809

MILLIE GAGE

Bear artist Millie Gage spent most of her life in the Susquehanna Valley region of New York where she worked for a major computer company. In 1981 a private donor purchased flowering plants for a village beautification project. The town's children planted and maintained the flowers. Millie enjoyed the children's enthusiasm and wanted to see the project continued, so she made two 3-foot bears. One was raffled to pay for the 1982 flowers; the other is kept in a place of honor in Millie's home.

After her retirement in July of 1991, Millie had much more time to devote to her "hobby." Millie began to design beautiful outfits that help emphasize the character of her bears.

After making bears for about ten years, Millie searched for a way to make her bears more easy to pose. Normal armatures were just not working for her. She decided to design her own. Millie took her idea to Hilfigers, a small company in her community. The flexlimbs were perfected and are used by many bear artists today.

Recently Millie has been involved in helping Ross Park Zoo raise funds to bring Humboldt penguins to New York.

Gage Bears
18 Ford Street
Windsor, NY 13865
607-655-2279

LYNN GATTO

Lynn has always been interested in making a wide range of crafts, as well as putting on Christmas craft shows. A friend invited her to attend an all Teddy Bear Show and from there Lynn turned her interest into just making bears. After designing her first patterns and making all the bears in acrylic, she attempted her first show. It was shortly after that show that Lynn discovered mohair and now she uses nothing else.

Her husband Phil has also taken an interest in teddy bears. He traces and cuts for her as well as helping to joint the bears.

"Because of Limerick Bear I have met many wonderful people and traveled to many different places in the United States and Europe."

Limerick Bear, Inc.
59 Jones Road
Wallingford, CT 06492
203-265-0757

SUSAN REDSTREAKE GEARY

At the age of 29, having been diagnosed with rheumatoid arthritis, Susan Redstreake Geary needed a profession she could pursue at home. Bear making and quilting seemed to fit the bill. Winner of numerous national awards for her original pictorial quilts, she has designed for America's top quilt magazines and taught classes in quilt making.

Susan was invited to make bears for the Disneyland Doll & Bear Show where her big sheepdog pulling a wagon load of teddy bears brought the highest price of any artist-made bear set at the show. Susan's bears have been nominated for many awards including a TOBY and Golden Teddy award in 1995.

Specializing in one-of-a-kind bears and very limited editions, Susan makes about 200 bears a year. She does all of the work on her bears herself.

Susan and her husband Joe recently published their first children's book about bears, *Best Friends Forever*. Their daughter Jennifer drew the wonderful illustrations. This book was such a success that a sequel is now in progress.

N.M. Bear Paws
2 Trueman Ct.
Baltimore, MD 21244
410-298-8459

MARY GEORGE

Mary's interest in teddy bears began in 1986 when her youngest child was a year old. At that time, she and her husband had embarked on the task of redecorating their home in a more early-American or country theme. While investigating ways in which to use antiques and collectibles in home decorating books at the library, Mary came across a book about antique bears. It was love at first sight and she knew she had to have some "old" bears for her home.

After pricing the "old" bears, Mary's husband Bill suggested that she make a bear that looked like the old bears she had fallen in love with.

Mary was on her way to making her teddy bears. She began researching antique bears and was soon designing patterns that incorporated the features of these old bears.

Mary makes all of her bears totally by herself and she will make only one bear at a time. She feels that each of her teddy bears is like one of her children and needs her undivided attention from the moment she traces him onto his fabric until he smiles at her when he's finished.

Mary George Bears
46713 Camelia Drive
Canton, MI 48187
313-453-6814

FRANCES HARPER

Frances began making teddy bears as a whim. She always loved to create things. Her background for 25 years was floral design. In 1988, she decided it was time to change careers. With her sideline of antique buying and selling, she started picking up teddy bears. She was even lucky enough to find some Stieffs.

Christmas was coming and she had a friend she wanted to get something special for. She decided to make her a teddy bear. As with most other bear artists, after that first bear, she was hooked.

Frances still remains faithful to the old-world style teddy that attracted her eight years ago. She signs the foot pads with "apple of my eye" bears.

"I feel so blessed that the events that happened in my life eight years ago have led me on this path. The friends I have made, the places that I have traveled, would never have been if it weren't for this crazy little fellow we call a teddy bear."

apple of my eye
233 Main Avenue
So. Hampton, NH 03827
603-394-7927

JERRIE KELLER

Ten years ago, Jerrie's children gave her a bear making class as a Mother's Day gift. Jerrie had always loved crafts, but had never made a bear. She ended up selling that first bear and was addicted to making more bears.

"My habit was so infectious that my husband started giving me ideas and helping me with jointing and stuffing. He is my number one assistant and critic."

Jerrie is best known for her cowboy bear. He wears his handmade cowboy attire, has a mustache and rides a wooden rocking horse. In 1989, while in California,

Jerrie was fortunate enough to meet Roy Rogers in his museum. He loved her bear so much that she traded him one of her bears for a hug and a picture. "I owe him for all the bear sales that picture and story have generated."

"We enjoy going to the teddy bear shows and have made many new friends who are more like family. Teddy bear collectors are very special people."

Jerrie's Thread Bears
8236 Fernwood Dr.
Norfolk, VA 23518
804-588-6222

KELLI KILBY

Miniature bear artist Kelli Kilby has been making bears for about sixteen years. She originally started off with larger bears.

In 1983, she began working as a dispatcher for the Los Angeles Police Department, answering the 911 lines and assigning radio calls. During the slow periods, she would work on bears. It seemed like the more stressful the calls got, the harder those bears would be stuffed!

In 1990, the stress of dispatching became too much, so her husband persuaded her to stay home and concentrate on her bear making career. Kelli joined a club that was making miniature bears. After trying her hand at miniatures she found that whenever she put small bears on her table, no one paid attention to her larger bears. She decided that she enjoyed the miniatures the best and has been making them ever since.

Kelli has been nominated for many awards including three TOBY awards and a Golden Teddy Award in 1995.

Kelli's Kollectibles
P.O. Box 2824
Rancho Cucamonga, CA 91729
909-980-3887

124

CAROL E. KIRBY

As a little girl, Carol was taught to sew by her mother. She put great emphasis on quality over quantity and speed, making Carol rip out and redo whatever was not done right and well. This lesson has been Carol's foundation throughout all her creative endeavors.

After raising three daughters, in 1988 Carol began collecting teddy bears from miniature figurines to all other varieties. Little did she know this would change the course of her life.

Carol's bears are designed and made entirely by the artist.

In 1994, she designed an unjointed teddy bear pattern for a craft book entitled *Sew It Tonight, Give It Tomorrow*. Her latest endeavor is to design for Ganz, a company based in Canada.

For Carol, her bears are a worldwide symbol of love and friendship, and her wonderful husband and three beautiful grown daughters give her the loving support she needs to put in the endless hours she loves! "God certainly gets the final credit for putting this in my life for which I am eternally grateful."

Kirby Bears
85 Harvard Rd.
Watervliet, NY 12189-1210
518-273-8872

MARGE KNAPP

Having a sense of humor and making teddy bears goes hand-in-hand for Marge. "Bears evoke a playful and carefree spirit. You can't take the world so seriously when you're holding a teddy bear."

"The world of bear making is very creative and the people I've met through this creative journey have brought me great joy. I can honestly say I haven't met a nasty bear-lover. There is a power that bears hold that goes right to the heart."

Marge has been making bears for approximately nine years. Before that she made folk art dolls for eight years.

Marge has just produced a 1996 Teddy Bear Calendar with Harris Publications of New York City. Placing her bears in whimsical settings for each month was a challenging but a most rewarding project.

Marge feels teddy bear making is "heart work"! Each one is an individual, having its own personality. Their warmth and tender nature is given freely to anyone who will open their heart.

Creative Thinking
5-29 First Street
Fair Lawn, NJ 07410
201-796-2332

MARY J. KOLAR

Mary started collecting bears several years ago and always thought how lucky the artists were to be able to create such wonderful, lovable bears.

Three years ago, she decided to try one for herself. Her first bears left a lot to be desired but they do have permanent homes with her three daughters.

After much experimenting, she finally got the look she wanted. Mary feels her bears are unique and show a true part of herself.

Mary has discovered that making bears is a full time job.

When she is not designing new furry friends, she is sewing, stuffing or putting on the finishing touches. To her it is all worthwhile when someone comes to her table and says they cannot live without one of her bears, and takes it home to be loved.

Mary enjoys meeting with other bear artists and sharing ideas, friendships and dreams.

Pochung Mountain Bears
29 Lauren Lane
Sussex, NJ 07461
201-875-8301

CARLA KULKA

From the time Carla was a child, she has always had some form of sewing needle in her hands. Knitting was a good portion of her life from eight years old to her late twenties. She loved knitting and could knit patterns without looking. She could even talk, count and chew gum at the same time.

Next she took up quilting. Carla received thirteen ribbons for her quilting projects. It seemed like everything she quilted had a heart in some form. This was brought to her attention by someone who had seen a lot of her work. She told them about a quilt that she was making for her daughter that was flowers. "It doesn't have hearts," she told them.

The next time she picked up the quilt to work on it, she noticed in the center of the flower was a heart.

Later, that wonderful needle stitched something spectacular. A BEAR! People tell Carla they like her bears because they "Have A Heart." "Yes, now I know what I was meant to do with the needle I used when I was but a child, make people smile. A greater appreciation cannot be found."

Have A Heart
3337 Concord Dr.
Brunswick, OH 44212-3131
216-273-1288

GINNY RATHELL

If you've ever been to a teddy bear show then you know how overwhelming it can be. Picture a banquet size room with table after table filled with wonderful bears of all sizes and shapes. Then imagine being there with no money in your wallet. Well, if you're someone like Ginny who has always loved making things, you hunt up a pattern and fabric and make your own bear. Pretty soon, with a little help from her friend, Marji, Ginny started experimenting with her own patterns.

Ginny enjoys making different styles of bears. Most of her bears are small--nine inches or so--but she does other sizes too. Her most recent bear is 19 inches. The first important part is a good head with a nice face, then a body to fit the head, then just the right ribbon or accessory. Then the real challenge--a name!

Ginny loves going to the shows. "I really enjoy doing the shows and meeting the people who buy my bears, personally. I've really met some great people through bear-making, on both sides of the table and look forward to meeting many more."

Ginnys Teddys
37 Bunting Lane
Naperville, IL 60565
708-355-2488

MARCIA SIBOL

Growing up as an only child, dolls and bears were a most important part of Marcia's life. As a young child she began sewing clothes for her dolls and designing clothing for paper dolls.

In 1982, Marcia met a bear collector and gave him one of her small thread-jointed bears. His enthusiasm led her to make her first properly jointed bear, Barnaby, and to become a bear collector.

Marcia came to love the old bears as well as bears of other artists. She particularly likes bears with life-like attributes.

In order to fully develop her bears' personalities, she began to design and produce costumes for them. The awards she has won and the encouragement received have led her to make a line of exclusively dressed bears as well as the traditional teddy bears.

"To me, my bears are very personal. I work on each one as an individual, letting its personality come through."

Bar Harbor Bears
P.O. Box 498
Bear, DE 19701
302-368-0012

LEEANN M. SNYDER

Like many other artists, Leeann stumbled into bear making. She had been receiving bear magazines for several years, looking at bear after bear, each more wonderful than the other!

Past crafting experiences had left Leeann burned out and frazzled, but after the creation of her first bear, she was truly hooked!

While working as a manager at a dress shop, Leeann began planning to attend a local Christmas craft show. The dress shop closed, and Leeann was in the bear business full time.

Leeann takes great pains to ensure smooth, unique noses. She soft-sculpts each mouth with a needle and thread to give greater dimension and finishes the eyes in the same way.

Although selling through shops and advertising in *Teddy Bear Review* helps her volume, she really enjoys selling direct to the customer the most. "Watching the love bloom between bear and human is a special moment I cherish. If I'm not at your local show, I'm just a phone call away."

Busser Bears
320 S. Fourth St.
Upper Sandusky, OH 43351
419-294-4823

JON & LIN VAN HOUTEN & JULIE LENGLE

Jon and Lin began collecting old bears while living in England in 1987 and 1988. It wasn't long before they tried their hand at making a teddy of their own.

They returned to the States in 1988 with a delightful little collection of antique bears and a really silly handful of home-made friends.

Using a room in their over 150-year-old cottage as "home" for this gathering of questionable characters, they decided this was the place where discarded creatures could come and be loved. They named their room "The Land of Merry Lights."

In 1994, Jon retired from his work in security and they moved their home and business into a log cabin, part of which dates to 1820, just outside Nashville, Tennessee.

"The return for our work has been the wealth of friends we have made along the way, the chance to travel, and the pure satisfaction of giving form to the creatures in our hearts and then seeing them loved by others as well."

The Land of Merry Lights
153 Denton Allen Rd.
Ashland City, TN 37015
615-299-0399

BONNIE WINDELL

Bonnie cannot remember a time when she wasn't sewing and creating things. Her grandmother taught her to embroider, and later to sew clothes for her dolls. By the age of 12, her mother refused to buy her any more stuffed animals since she felt her room had reached its maximum capacity. Bonnie decided she would have to make her own. She discovered commercial patterns and made a dog, frog and turtle.

After the birth of five children, Bonnie turned to her sewing skills to clothe them. Later, wishing to earn extra money and still be at home with her children, she looked for a creative outlet. She entered a teddy bear contest in a local craft store.

Even though she lost the contest, she became addicted to making teddy bears.

In 1990, Bonnie won her first national award from *Teddy Bear Review* magazine, a Golden Teddy Award for a miniature bear.

Bonnie does her own photography including the one we've chosen to share.

Windlewood
6611 Red Horse Pike
Newburgh, IN 47630
812-858-9299

SALLY WINEY

Sally's dream was to have a career in social work, helping other people. She was unable to finish college, and ended up married with three lovely children. In 1976, as a young wife and mother, she found herself with very little money but a lot of creativity. Sally began making stuffed animals for her kids and as gifts for friends in order to save on the high cost of toys.

This worked out so well that she decided she might be able to make some money without leaving her home. Sally's business boomed. Orders were piling up. Fortunately, her husband Bill realized that Sally needed help.

He quit his job as a trucking company executive to run the house, care for the children and support Sally in her bear-making venture.

Sally has made limited editions of bears to be sold for a variety of AIDS and battered children's organizations.

This year Sally was nominated for a Golden Teddy Award for her tiny, cuddly Cuzzy Ken Bear.

Winey Bears
P.O. Box 7
St. Peters Village, PA 19470
610-469-1020

THE TEDDY BEAR MUSEUM OF NAPLES

This wonderful bear museum was founded by Mrs. Frances Pew Hayes. Since her family was so large, they decided to draw names for gifts Christmas of 1984. Her five-year-old grandson drew her name. Not having a clue what to buy his grandmother, he asked her what she wanted.   She answered that she was always needing rubber bands and paper clips. Now even a five-year-old knew that this was not a proper Christmas gift. He asked her for another idea and since it was the Chinese Year of the Bear, that's what she asked for!

From this snugly "M & M" bear given as a Christmas present, a teddy bear collection and this museum were born.

Mrs. Hayes was absolutely thrilled by her little furry friend, and soon she became a true "arctophile." As she traveled, she began to buy teddy bears. Also now everyone knew what to buy for her. Soon there were bears and "bearaphrenalia" of all sizes and shapes. As the collection grew, there were many requests from people of all ages to see the collection. Thus, the idea of and need for the museum was born.

The doors of The Teddy Bear Museum of Naples were opened to the public as a not-for-profit public corporation on December 19, 1990 by "Frannie," 1,500 donated bears, the staff and volunteers. Since then, between 35,000 and 50,000 visitors per year have enjoyed seeing and hearing the variety of teddys in residence.

The museum displays the work of more than 400 artists, bears of most current major manufacturers, and at least one bear each of many of the other manufacturers. Each bear wears a numbered inventory tag. A sign is displayed which gives the company name, artist/designer, city, state and country of origin.

Museum director George B. "Brownie" Black, Jr. states: "My goal is to make the museum the central source for information about Teddy Bear lore, artists, manufacturers and their creations." He adds: "This is one of the few places I've ever worked or been where virtually 100 percent of the people walk out smiling."

The museum is located at 2511 Pine Ridge Road in Naples, Florida 33942. I'm sure they would be delighted to see you!

GOOD BEARS OF THE WORLD

What or who is Good Bears of the World? I will quote from *Bear Tracks*, which is the Journal of the Good Bears of the World: "Good Bears are people who come from a variety of backgrounds, professions and ages, sharing an interest in giving, aiding and comforting in a quiet, low-key fashion. Good Bears have special feelings for children and elderly people and know how a teddy bear helps soften the harshness of this world. Good Bears' hearts are open and are not 'exclusive,' but 'inclusive,' with the aim to put the comfort of a teddy bear into the arms and hearts of every traumatized child or lonely, forgotten adult in the world. Good Bears can and do make a difference."

Madmen inflicted havoc with lives and souls one day in Oklahoma City. The next day the largest single shipment of Good Bears ever sent to one destination were delivered into the crisis scene where no one else was permitted to go. These bears were dispensed at the church where relatives, friends and children waited for word of survivors. These bears were sent from the Tulsa den, which was the closest GBW den.

Good Bears of the World showed the same generosity to the earthquake victims in Kobe, Japan. Good Bears did more than give comfort to Japan with bears; they also helped to build the relatively new art of "charity" in Japan. Good Bears of the World are always ready and willing to pitch in and help spread some happiness whenever and wherever there is a need.

Good Bears of the World has no subsidy or regular means of support. Its work is accomplished solely with income from membership fees and donations. Officers and board members serve without pay and depend on volunteers for assistance.

If you wish to donate or assist in some way with this worthwhile, international cause while helping people feel energized by the gift of teddy bears, please write the national headquarters:

Good Bears of the World
P.O. Box 13097
Toledo, Ohio 43613-0097
or call 419-531-5365

BIBLIOGRAPHY

BOOKS:

Greene, Carol
Margarete Steiff, Toy Maker   Childrens Press
                                                    Chicago, IL

Hebbs, Pam
Collecting Teddy Bears   Pincushion Press
                                                    Tampa, FL